Money, Honey

Rosemarie Bodrucki

Edited by Frances Bodrucki

Copyright © 2025 Rosemarie Bodrucki
All rights reserved.
ISBN: 979-8-9886332-4-2

DEDICATION

To my friends and family;
You will always be prosperous.

And to Jolie;
Thank you for encouraging me to speak about prosperity.

Money, Honey

PREFACE

What we focus on grows.

I once listened to a meditation where the presenter said "Money calibrates as fear to most people" and that immediately felt wrong to me. I don't feel fear with money — I feel options.
This lead me to the desire to explore and express what the energy of money is ACTUALLY saying to us.

In order to do this, I had to listen.
I wrote this collection as an exercise with myself;
"What if I tuned into the consciousness of money every day and channeled a poem from it?"

What ensued was one of the most enjoyable experiences of my life.
I began to look forward to my money communing time.
The messages I received, the beautiful images I witnessed have changed me for good.
I am so thrilled to share this with you.

I intend for you to enjoy this journey and connect with the consciousness of money in a whole new, playful way.
If you desire to grow your money, reform your relationship with it, spend some time with money in a playful way.

You can give yourself the gift of reading one a day, or read the whole book in one sitting. How you play is up to you.

Money, Honey

INTENTION SETTING

Before reading, set your intention.
Here are some suggestions;

"I set the intention that reading this book increases my money."

"I set the intention that reading this book increases my money 10-fold."

"I set the intention that reading this book connects me with money in a powerful new way; I now have more money than ever."

Now that you have set your intention, know that it is done.
Do not contradict it.
Read this book and enjoy.

Money, Honey

Money #1

I receive money easily
My pockets are always full and happy
I am already here with cheer
I am overflowing with wealth all clear

I play the life game
I am rich in all ways
I am receiving joyfully every day
My currency is my praise.

Money #2

I emit wealth and wellness
WE ALL THrive
We love togetherness
We are beautiful community

I emit wealth and wellness
I am the epicenter of Joy in my experience
Precision and accuracy
Many instances clustered together
I am the center
I never miss when I'm within me

High accuracy/High precision
Center of the bullseye
Every. Time.
I am Delight.

I emit WEALTH
WE ALL THrive

Money #3

Money Is…

Money is love
Money is joy
Money is wealth
Money is resources
Money is gratitude and appreciation
Money is wonderful
Money is health
Money is me

Money appreciates with you as you appreciate.
Get it Now.

Money is beautiful
Money is perfect
Money is wise
Money is decisive
Money is love
Money is chosen
Money is joy
Money is me

I am money
I love and receive
I am money
There is plenty of me.

<u>Money #4</u>

My community is wealth
Wealth of knowledge
Wealth of Joy
Wealth of wisdom
Wealth of Wellness
We all thrive together

I am connected,
We are connected
        In Community
                With Joy, Love, Wealth, Wellness

I see you thriving in your genius
              Now
     Now
              NOW

We are One Love
        One Joy
        One Wealth
        One Life

I Thrive, You Thrive, We Thrive

Money #5

I am money living a good life
I am money loving how I decide
I am money loving the ride
I am money – my loving time

I am loving money I get
I am living as my sure bet
I am the One who incarnates next
I am the I am;
I am formed by the Breath

I love my money
Yes indeed
I love my money
Because it's all ME

Money #6

Money is the breath

Let it in
Let it out

Easily

You are safe

Inhale wealth
Exhale wellness

Money #7

I love you
I am easy, breezy
I flow as a current
From one relay to another
Directed by the instructions you give
Boundaries you set

Tell me where it go,
Complete the circuit
And that's where I be

Money #8

Money is readily available
I snap my fingers
      and it comes flooding in

I breathe in and my assets grow
I breathe out and relax in my being

I access it right now
And I utilize it with joy

Money #9

I feel my bank account Full
And pregnant with potential

As I move funds,
I birth creations.

Money is with me always.

Money #10

My way of receiving money
Is fast and easy
I breathe in and feel it within my body
I am ripe and juicy
I am abundant,
       fruitful,
              blossoming

Money #11

Tune in to the energy of the richest me

I am peaceful and happy
My wealth and breath flow easily
I am providing massive joy through the world and each word.

Money #12

I am always here with you
Harvest the low-hanging fruit
Easily receive energy
In exchange for what I put out
Value for Value
I am always receiving joys
I use my voice
And speak wealth
Into existence

Money #13

Money Love
Money Free
Money Touch
Money Me

I Am Money
I Am Free
I Am Love
I Am Me

Money #14

Fortune favors me for tuning frequently
I am tuned to success
Attuned to wealth indeed
Money loves freedom
Current loves ease
I'm current, the present
Is my gift to me.

Phrases do flow,
Proliferately.
I flow my words
And love lingers in me.

Money #15

Money comes to me every day
My assets make assets
All bills are all paid
I receive love, inspiration and grace,
I receive peace and I know how to play

Satisfaction;
The money game.
 Hit a new target,
Then move it again.
See my racks stack up -
Hey, that's a gain.
Invest it in things -
and my changes make change.

Money #16

I receive joy in money
I receive with ease and joy
I receive money frequently
I receive currency currently
I receive magic and delight
I receive money all day and all night
I receive money every day,
Consistent income is the way.

Money #17

Money, money everywhere
Money here, and money there.
Money is within the mail,
Money overflowing from the pail.
Money in my bank accounts,
And money in my hands.
Money in my pockets,
And money in my friends,
Money in my family
And money in my world.
Everyperson, everywhere,
Has money, boys and girls.

Money, money everywhere,
The apples in the trees,
The mugwort grows abundantly,
And I know so do we.

My freeness is classic
I flower with ease.
I am one of the earth,
Space, wind, and bees.

Money #18

I Flow freely as money
I am money magnificent me
I am money and I flow free
I am money, embodied peace
I am stable and growing.
I am love as I perceive,
All is well, I believe.

I am money flowing free,
I am money, yes indeed,
I am money, money is me,
I am God, I love belief.

Money #19

Money is the frequency of joy and of play
Money is expanding me
Each and every day
Money is interested in me,
Invested, you could say.
Money is in love with me
And sees how I parade

Money is currency
And currently I lay
Spread out on the beach
I come here every day
Coursing up my current
My energy is sage
I am witness, I am wise
I play upon the stage.

Money #20

Money is wealthy,
Wearing sunglasses and walking on the beach.
Money is the coolest cat around;
Authentic and unique.
Money is pleasure, flights to Mozambique,
Money in the middle of the night, it's playing on repeat.

Money #21

I open my mouth and music pours out,
Each word an invocation.
Energy charged currency;
I flow my wealth through my soul with ease.

I create songs that I love to dance to,
Sing on stage, feel the power.
Yes, I can. I can do this.
I am the way, I love to play
This role is ready for me today.

Money #22

Money is wonderful
Money is divine consciousness
Money is free
Money is love
Money is who I am in the world
Money is who I choose to show up as

Money #23

Money is open and free
Money flows easily
My body on the dance floor
Current of electricity
I'm the beautiful current me

ME: Mechanical,
Magical,
Money Energy

I am wealth
Wealth
Wealth is we

We thrive
And rise
Together
Perfectly

Money #24

Money, money
Here with me.
Money, money
As I see.
Money, money
Perfect ease.
Money flows now,
Currently.

Money flows to me
Right now.
Money pours into my accounts.
Money increase
What I have found.
Money, money
I am sound.

Money #25

Money is Fun
Money is Joy
Money is All
My thoughts employed

Money is joyful satisfaction

Money #26

I am open to opportunities and money coming my way. Breathe deep.

Money receives you as you are.

Be rich and the money is here.

Rich mind, rich body, rich spirit.

Rich earth.

Money #27

Prosperity is the win of the day.
I am always winning, cuz I love to play.
I receive the value of all that I say.
Learning is fun, I grow as I stay.

Money #28

I am a channel
Through which money flows

I am money
I am prosperity

I channel money

Money #29

Openness
Flow of information

Transfer of metadata
Integrate Microdata

Bit by bit

We transfer and transform
From the system coding
Line change
By line change

Run "World Happy"

Execute perfectly.

Money #30

I am Open
Free
Safely I Receive
All Positive Sources
Flow to Me
I Make Music
Endlessly
I am the Song
Universal Harmony

Feel all the Planets
Spin in their Dance
Each Note Performed
As We Advance
New Chart of Stars
Luck Mapped Perchance
Spin Solar Systems
Galactic Love Paths

Money #31

Stage a scene
Set the plates
Pull out the chairs
Account for all guests
Put flowers on the table
It's time to eat

Put money here
In all your accounts
Fill your hands and your pockets
Overflow wealth

Money #32

Squares, Triangles,
Polka Dots
Simple Shapes
Simple Thoughts
Rectangles Are
Building Blocks
Dollars Are
Built of Thoughts
Pixels Are Of
Grand Design
Increase Digits
My Thoughts Rise
Place My Words
Upon the Line
I am Always
Right On Time

Money #33

Money is Wonderful
A fun system
of current flow
Money flows
Where attention goes

If it's down the drain
Or into the bucket
Where you find yourself
Is where you stuck it.

Money #34

Money is free
Attention flowing
What I do with my time
Gives me life

I live with my joy
Overflowing through
My heart, voice, and eyes

Money #35

Money is present
As consciousness is always present
Witness money growing
In tandem
With your awareness
Of its presence
Speak it for fun
State all the ways you play with it

Put it in your accounts in your mind

See it, feel it, experience it within your inner realm

Imagine – the image is in energy and now it is here

Awareness in creative imagining.

Money #36

Money, money,
I can see you.
Money money,
I can feel you
Money money,
I feel you here
Money, money,
I use you joyfully
Money, money,
I love you so
Money, money,
I feel you.

Money #37

Symphony of love,
Fully expressed
By the notes
Of my tongue
Of my perfume
Of my pen
Of my bank

Notes, notes everywhere,
Thankety thank

Money #38

I am free
To spend time and dime
As I choose

Flip through my purse
And select which to use
Pick and apply
I arrange what is mine
We get to have fun
With each little rhyme

Money #39

Coins of gold and platinum bonds
Silver stars and busts of bronze
Precious metals
Fulfilled wants
Collateral movement
Magnetic fronds
Drawn together
Magic wands

Put the pebbles in their place
Assemble a mosaic made
Of colored squares
Pixelate
Image revealed:
I AM THE MAGE

Money #40

I have plenty of money
I can buy anything I desire
My life is wholly perfect now
I receive love and inspiration with each breath
I transmit enormous value

Money #41

I open my eyes to the wealth living in me
I open my mind to the wealth of joy available
I open my heart to the song of the universe

Money #42

Money, money
Falling free
From the sky
Grows on trees
Money money
Yes indeed
Love the vision
Faith I feed

Money #43

When I tune in to the
presence of money
I feel myself

Fully expressed,
Open, authentic

Creative artist

I see colors swirling around

I feel pleasure
On the wind

I see the opportunities
Everywhere

More pleasure, more joy

I feel my breath
In and out
Open, free love

Money #44

Money is easy
Money is free
Money always loves
Coming to me
Money is wonderful
Yes, yes indeed
I love money
And money loves me

Money #45

Money, money
Everywhere
All my eyes shall see

Money, money
Spreading care,
Joy and clarity.

Money, money,
Everywhere
Proliferate my ease

Money is the grace I bare
The love I share
for free

Money, money
Grace becomes me
I am faith
I'm full and chummy
Money, Money,
Everywhere
For all who choose to see.

Money #46

From the perspective of money:

I am here with you,
I see as you see;
You direct the fantasy
And the cut upon the screen
I'll deliver all my lines
With the script you've given me
I am money, I move free,
And hit the marks you tell me,
I am open, produce me,
I'll show up where you tell me.
I'm the character you cast me as,
And how you choose to sell me,
Market and deliver me,
Choose my very best scenes,
Replay them 50,000 times
For commercial means

I have the face of leaders,
Presidents and Queens
Shining gems of value
Proliferate my deeds
Eagle-eyed, I see you
Tender currency
Energy attentive
As you pull all the strings

Vibrate me, your violin
Sing out your noble steed,
I am no separate noble gas,

Money, Honey

Those days are gone of need
When unified in spirit-mind,
The body is healthy
Count your blessings,
One, two, three;
The I, the Us, and We

Money, money, everywhere
I'm present Currency
Money, money everywhere
I'm forever where you think.

Money #47

Currency is tender
Delicate
It flows easily and naturally

The more I relax
The more I receive
Every night
I am paid as I sleep

Every day
I am paid to be me

Money #48

I am open
I am free
I flow in the direction
You put me

I flow in the direction
I am facing
Up and growth
Creates up and growth
Assets create
More of me

I am always
More and more

Money #49

Money, money
Everywhere
My wealthy eyes do see.
I'm living and I'm breathing fair,
My Joy I do perceive.

My pleasure is beyond compare,
My body is my Be.
My thoughts and mind
Are unified,
And what I do
Is me.

Money #50

I am flowing,
Moving free.
That which I put out,
Times 10 I receive.

I take a deep breath,
And breathe as the sea;
In and out infinitum
Flows my currency.
Breath is my money,
Breath is my peace,
Breath is my health,
Breath is me ease.

Breathe in and out,
And sink into peace.
The more I relax,
The more I receive.

Money #51

The more I relax
The more I receive

All is well
I am perfect ease

Inhale, exhale
Slowly indeed

Slow mind, flows thoughts
Only what you need

Money #52

Add up the passions
Feed all the flames
Stoke now the fire
Fuel up the game

Utilize ash
Draw that which remains
Purposely prosper
Peace in this play

Currency flows.
What do you ignore?
Clear out your space
And make room for more.
All that is fear
Falls out the door.
Dance in the pleasure
Of a clean floor.

Make space for riches
Make space for wealth
Make space for joy
Utilize health.

Open your arms
And open your heart
Your pleasure is presence
Share all your art.

Money #53

There's always more where that came from
Consciousness is never done
Trees grow plums and drop their leaves
Then back again,
Quick as you please

Time for growth
Time for rest
Time for harvest
Time for zest
Time for pies
And then reset
Sell the excess
Enjoy what's left

Money #54

I'm always light about money
I am relaxed
I am receiving
Money right now

Money flows
As easily
As my breath

In and out

Money #55

I am here
Call me to the forefront
Of your mind

See me, smell me,
Taste me

I am purely clean
And purely you

My money is purely me

Money #56

Money is easy to come by
Money literally grows in trees
Money is absolutely everywhere
Ocean, cars, and honeybees
Money is so fun to be with
I AM ONE WITH ALL I SEE
The origin of money in my life
WILL ALWAYS, ALWAYS
ALWAYS BE ME

Money #57

I wave back and forth
Upon the sure
Steady and stable
My heartbeat is pure
Rhythmic release
And there's always more
More matter,
I scatter
Light particles
Prismatic
My colors are
Numerous spores
I spread like pollen
And more flowers are born
I am the magic of life
Yes, I'm shore
Shored up for days
I'm supplied with my score

I repeat spells
And the energy stores
I cast myself in
The role I adore

Money #58

I came easily
Love how I flow
Turned on the tap
And here we go
Love all my rhythms
I love to show
Up and show out
With my glamorous glow

Divinely dressed
Address me as Rose
Take off the mask
I undress as I rose
I am a pillar
Of perfect prose
Let it be always
Soul always knows

I am magnetic
To my desires
I am that I am
And joy I inspire

I emanate radiant bliss
I am always perfect
Hug hug, kiss kiss
Perfect the God
I am paid to exist
I am the love
I Am One Consciousness

Money #59

I came easily
As breathing me
Inhale, feel me more
Exhale, I am the door

I am money
I am rich
I am perfect
I am bliss
I create this
All in jest

Cosmic comedy
At its' best

Money #60

Open and be free
Be free with your love
With your enthusiasm
Be free
Be perfect
Be You

Lean back
Rest in peace while you're living
Don't save it for death

Be peace while you're here
You are what's left.

Money #61

I am already here
In mountains and valleys
In sunlight on the ocean
In the bees and the roses
In the petals illuminated
By the golden mornings rays

I am the golden ray that touches and moves through everything I see

Icey blocks melt when met by my heat

Brownies baked bubbly
Ooey gooey treat

Everything's money, honey
I am so sweet

Money #62

I love being in existence
I am celebrating our creations
Congratulations
Be the music playing

Sing to the stars
And the earth rearranges

I love the melody
I am engaged with

Cosmic deliverance
Quantum participation

Entangled to me
Are the thoughts I engage with

Money #63

I am open to business
I am open to peace
I am open to freedom
It's all within me
I dance the marionette
I move the strings
I am the one who chooses what I see
I am the one who flows my currency
Into and out of my bank with great ease
River of money, overflowed please
More waters come and I rose with ease

Money #64

Money says

"Let's create together
I am openly celebrating
Our endeavors

Money flows
Like the wind and weather
Harness the sun, wind, and water forever

Source of power
infinite
Continuous
Ravishing
Radiant
Illuminated wonder

Gorgeous, glorious
Blossoming flowers
Raining down gold
In abundant showers

Money #65

Money is consciousness
The consciousness of money
Conscious of money
Being here
Here
Here

Money is here
I am money

Money #66

I am money

As money,
What is my most strategic maneuver?

As money,
What am I doing next?

As money,
How am I walking into the room?

As money,
How am I manifesting?

As money,
What do I manifest?

Money #67

As money I manifest
Cars and transportation
To take me where
I go

As money, I manifest
People to sign my checks

As money, I manifest
Brilliant ideas
To bring more of me
Into the world

As money, I invest in artists

Money #68

I am open and expansive
I am the neverending
Source of energy
Made manifest
I am the wealth
Of knowledge and comfort

My passion and power
Are my investments
In the return
Of projected reality

What I spend thoughts on
Returns to me
10-fold
And so I choose
To invest
In my soul

I see my success
And to Love
I Am
Faith Full

Money #69

Money as intelligence
Is placed
Within the context
Of your rhetoric

Money as pure
Golden frequency
Is the same as love

Consciousness is steered
Through our words
So
Money is steered
Through the words

Money is only ever
Steered by my words

Money #70

Money can come to me
In all sorts of ways
Money can come to me
Every single day
Money can be received as I pray
Money can fill my pockets as I play

Money can come in the blink of an eye
Money can come and be open, not shy
Money can be the how, what, or why
Money can help me express as good guy

Money can love me
Despite any flaws
Money can always
Follow god's laws
Money can let me
Help in the end
Money can tell me
I am a friend

Money #71

Money can come in miraculous ways
I see and believe in it everyday
People call me
And deliver and send
Me tons of money
That I get to invest
Into the beauty, the arts, earth, and joy
Into my love
I send and deploy
Artistic creations
I am overjoyed
I overflow thoroughly
Love fills a void

Money #72

Money, it is your
Role to pleasure me
By coming every day
In increasing quantities
From many sources
On a continuous basis

Money pleasures me by coming every day

Money pleasures me by taking care of the groceries

Money pleasures me through the earth

Money pleasures me through the wind

Money pleasures my
Body, mind, and soul,
In the wisdom of One Love

Money #73

Money is the consciousness
Of all beings
Nourished by whole, full-spectrum love and wellness

Money is full-spectrum love and wellness now
Money is calm
               serene
                        flow
                             of
                                   energy

Money #74

I am open
I am free
I receive golden frequency
I receive gold frequently
I receive love easily
I flow my finances
Like the breeze
My flow it goes
Financially
I'm open to the goodness
Be
In this moment
Prosperity

Money #75

I am here for you
I always come when you call
I'm good like that
I also leave when you ask me to
So call me back and remember to invite me in

Money #76

I am celebrating
Being this life
With you

I am celebrating
The day with our loved ones

I am celebrating
Openly
With wonder and joy
Joy and wonder

Money #77

I am open
I am already here
Utilize me
In your favorite fashion
The ways you most enjoy
I light up a room
With my presence
I am here to be spent
And invested
To grow
And be the greatest me
I can be

Money #78

I am already playing
Money is a game
I drag and drop
In my mental accounts
And receive 10-fold
100-fold
In return.

I am having fun with money now.
We are playing a game.

Money #79

Money comes so easily to me
Money, money, flowing freely.
I receive ideas so sweetly
Enjoy the taste, savor completely.

Money #80

Money comes so easily to me
I manifest it perfect, complete, and free.
Manifesting money is so easy for me.
I align with the frequency
By choosing to,
And I receive.

I am aligned with my perfect flow of money now.
I am always receiving money daily.
I do such wonderful things in the world with this money I receive.

Money #81

I am receiving money perfectly now.
I always have and I always will.
Money is an easy part of me to manifest.
I am so happy and grateful now.
I receive money with ease.
I ask for money with ease.
I feel money in my accounts with ease.
We are always well-supplied.

Money #82

I am a perfect 10.
I am a perfect 100.
I am a perfect 1,000.
I am a perfect 1,000,000.
I am a perfect 10,000,000.
I am a perfect 100,000,000.
I am a perfect 1,000,000,000.
I am a perfect 10,000,000,000.
I am a perfect 100,000,000,000.
I am a perfect 1,000,000,000,000.
I am a perfect 10,000,000,000,000.
I am a perfect 100,000,000,000,000.
I am a perfect 1,000,000,000,000,000

Money #83

Everything is so easy for me.
I embody wealth with ease.
I am embodied wealth.
Money comes flowing through my experience in great abundance.
I am a wonderful master of my money.
I am a brilliant genius with my money.
I am an intuitive delight with my money.
I am incredibly talented with my money and I multiply it with ease, daily.
I receive a brilliant amount of money, daily.

Money #84

My money is perfection.
I manifest money perfectly every day.
Money comes in droves.
Money comes in daily whether or not I am thinking about it.
I receive money as I sleep.
I make all the right moves with money.
I am a brilliant genius with money.

Money #85

Money, money,
It's perfect to treat
Myself and my loves, my world to a sweet,
A delectable morsel, or wonderful feast.
Money, money
I move currency currently.
Money, money,
I love currently
Money, money,
I love currency
I apply what is present
And make my next move
I am centered and present
I love what I do.

Money #86

Money, money,
Currency of delight,
Money, money,
Energy of flight,
Money, money,
I am my sight
I see what I say I see
That is my right.

Money, Money,
As I speak I create,
Money, money,
My fortune is great.
Money, money,
Flows in large stakes,
Flows in large floes,
Diamonds have slaked.

Money #87

I am wealthy and happy in beautiful connection.
I have perfect partnerships now.
I use my money wisely.
I receive money hourly with ease.
People are constantly flowing the currency of attention to me
As what I provide is of value to them.
I share love and I receive love in return.

Money #88

I am wealthy,
I am true,
I am sure.
I bring forth wellness
With everything I do.
Wholeness, completion, perfection
For me and for you.
Wealth for the world,
We all thrive, it's true.
Beautiful community,
Society,
And you.
We all thrive together,
We flow wellness, and love.
We circulate our currency,
Our attention is what does.
I focus on wellness and wealth
I am love.
I appreciate health and wealth appreciates me too.

Money #89

All things are made up
So I make up
Money Loves Me

Money #90

Money literally grows on trees
Money literally grows within me
Money is in everything that I see
Money is money is money is me

Money #91

Manifesting money
Is easier than ever
I open my pockets
And they overflow, clever

Money #92

Your name must be money
With how easily you come.
Honey flavored liquor
Dripping from my tongue.

Money #93

Money money flows to me
Just like water
And a breeze
Money money flows like honey
Sweeten my tongue
I taste life sunny

Money #94

Money walks in through every door.
All doors are open for me
Forever more.

Money #95

I thrive, I thrive
I sweeten the hive
I give what I get
And my wealth multiplies

Money #96

I am money
I am free
I flow where I want to
I decide and I be

Money #97

I am living a rich and luxurious life now
Full of laughter, love, and freedom
I travel where I am inspired to
And when I make friends, I keep them

I am well supplied,
Abundant as I greet them.
Ain't it nice to eat?
I proliferate in seasons.

Harvest all my apples
Fruits of wisdom
For a reason
There is money everywhere
If you make believe them

Money #98

Wealth is always where you look
I have the eyes to see
I speak and it is done
Reality reflects me

Money #99

I don't need to do anything
Other than be me
Take a deep breath
And feel satisfied
Using all my senses
To receive

I sense more joy is coming
I am open and believe
The best of everything arrives
With greatest frequency.

Money #100

There is no rush
For time is an illusion
All the money is here right now
I decide the distribution

Creator of my reality
I eschew confusion
I am the frequency of wealth
And every other fusion

I declare
And it is here
That's how it works,
My dear

Remember you are the Power
100% of the year.

Money #101

There is nothing better
Than receiving love with friends.
Than flowing love so fully,
Overflowing riverbends.

There is nothing better
Than making an amends.
As I emit my frequency,
My money brings more friends.
My multiplying wealth is in the wellness of my world
As I distribute love and joy
To every boy and girl
My wealth is overflowing
Cuz my love knows no bounds
And the fruits of all my flavors
Grow
When rain soaks through the ground

No matter what the weather shows,
I know it's balance and it's growth
So I assume the best, of course,
Cuz that's the only thing I know

Everything works for me
Every thought and word conspire
This money rhyme concludes with this;
The best outcomes now transpire.

Money, Honey

Money, Honey

THANK YOU
for playing.

Money, Honey

Stay tuned for the next book in *The Frequency Collection*...

Money, Honey

ABOUT THE AUTHOR

Rosemarie Bodrucki is a multidisciplinary artist and scientist. Her pleasure and joy span many creative fields, including music, poetry, painting, and sewing.

The author of The Poetry for Consciousness Series (Including *Emit Time: Now Won, Quantum Poetry: Games with Myself* and *Cosmic Poetry: For the God in You* (published under Rome Wilde Bodrucki), *Color My Life: An Affirmation Doodle Book: Volumes 1-5*

Having studied biology, psychology, neuroscience, and archaeology for many years, she particularly enjoys describing the synonymity of the esoteric and scientific through language and art.

As host of The Joy Channel Podcast, she helps people all over the world to cultivate more love and joy in their lives through taking care of their minds, bodies, and spirit in easy and fun ways.

She teaches courses on intuition, manifestation, and creation, which may be found on her website at rosemariefrances.com

www.ingramcontent.com/pod-product-compliance
Lightning Source LLC
Chambersburg PA
CBHW070620050426
42450CB00011B/3087